T0193494

JOYFULLY MARRIED

WestBow Press books may be ordered through
booksellers or by contacting:

WestBow Press
A Division of Thomas Nelson & Zondervan
1663 Liberty Drive
Bloomington, IN 47403
www.westbowpress.com
844-714-3454

ISBN: 978-1-6642-7286-6 (sc)
ISBN: 978-1-6642-7287-3 (e)

Library of Congress Control Number: 2022913171

Print information available on the last page.

WestBow Press rev. date: 08/16/2022

JOYFULLY MARRIED

Wisdom from Couples Married 50 or More Years

JEANNE CURCIO

WESTBOW
PRESS®
A DIVISION OF THOMAS NELSON
& ZONDERVAN

DEDICATION

This book is dedicated to my husband,
Lou, for our joyful years of marriage —
acting justly, loving tenderly, and walking
humbly together with our God (Mic 6:8).

GRATITUDE

My appreciation and admiration
go to Phil for his years
of friendship, skill, patience,
and belief in this project.

I am deeply grateful to Rose of Sharon,
my writing accountability partner,
for our weekly reviews and
prayers. Thank you. Write on!

My thanks also go out to
Valerie for her encouragement
and editorial review.

Joy: a deep feeling or condition of happiness or contentment[1]

CONTENTS

INTRODUCTION

The idea for this book came to me as I reflected on my parents' and my in-laws' marriages. Both couples had different life experiences, lived in different parts of the United States, and raised families of different sizes. How did they stay together through so many years and still find joy in being married, while other couples end up seeking a divorce?

I wanted to gain wisdom and insight from other couples about living a lasting, joyful marriage, not only for me and my husband but for all married couples. I decided to interview couples I knew, including relatives, friends, and acquaintances, who have been married for at least 50 years. I appreciate the time they spent with me and the wisdom about marriage that they shared with me. I asked each couple the same question to discover what was common among them and what was unique about them.

I hope that what I learned from them and have written will inspire and guide all married couples as they travel this journey of life together.

Keep reading to learn about the ways these couples have remained joyfully married and have kept Jesus' command that "Therefore, what God has joined together, no human being must separate" (Mt 19:6).

COUPLES MARRIED IN THE

1970s

Fill us at daybreak with
your mercy, that all our
days we may sing for joy.

PS 90:14

OTTO & JACKIE

Married 1973

WHAT HAS KEPT YOU JOYFULLY MARRIED FOR 50 OR MORE YEARS?

➤ Learning from our parents that "no matter what, you work it out."

➤ Having a true commitment to God and to each other and knowing that God is in the forefront.

➤ Pledging never to strike or curse at each other or put each other down.

➤ Having a partnership and being in the marriage together.

➤ Being very supportive of each other.

➤ Letting go of yesterday and taking care of today.

Even though Otto and Jackie hadn't yet reached their golden wedding anniversary at the time of this printing, they met as teenagers and dated for five years before getting married.

You have brought them abundant joy and great rejoicing.

IS 9:2

DAVID & PATRICIA

Married 1972

WHAT HAS KEPT YOU JOYFULLY MARRIED FOR 50 OR MORE YEARS?

- ► Sharing a common faith.

- ► Making wedding vows as a promise to each other and to God.

- ► Having the same values.

- ► "Everything we do as a family revolves around the church."

Go, eat your bread with
joy and drink your wine
with a merry heart,
because it is now that
God favors your works.

ECCL 9:7

JOHN & CASSANDRA

Married 1972

WHAT HAS KEPT YOU JOYFULLY MARRIED FOR 50 OR MORE YEARS?

- Taking time to get to know each other and dating for a couple of years before falling in love.

- Liking and enjoying being around each other.

- Double-dating with other friends.

- Having a shared faith, which is very important and central to family activities.

- Knowing that God is good and always has been.

Joy delights in joy...

SONNET XIII,
WILLIAM SHAKESPEARE[2]

MIKE & JANE

Married 1972

WHAT HAS KEPT YOU JOYFULLY MARRIED FOR 50 OR MORE YEARS?

- Honesty.

- "Give and take."

- Love.

- Respect.

- Never going to bed mad.

- Staying within financial means.

- Sharing interests and doing things together.

- Dancing.

- Skiing.

Mike's parents are Larry and Mary Lou (see page 55). Jane's parents (both deceased) were married 70 years.

And he brought
forth his people with
joy, and his chosen
with gladness.

PS 105:43 (DOUAY-RHEIMS BIBLE)

DCN. JAMES & CAROLINE

Married 1971

WHAT HAS KEPT YOU JOYFULLY MARRIED FOR 50 OR MORE YEARS?

- Being best friends.

- Having the same goals.

- "Gotta have a sense of humor and use lots of it."

- Thinking alike.

- "There will be no divorce."

- Waking up and making a daily decision to still be in love.

Then the just will
be glad; they will rejoice
before God; they will
celebrate with great joy.

PS 68:4

JACK & LORRIE

Married 1971

WHAT HAS KEPT YOU JOYFULLY MARRIED FOR 50 OR MORE YEARS?

- Believing that God brought about the marriage.

- Having faith.

- Being friends first.

- Seeing the Holy Spirit's presence in family life.

- Having gratitude for blessings.

- Acknowledging each other's gifts and weaknesses.

- Being committed to each other through diffi-cult times.

I give you a new commandment: love one another. As I have loved you, so you also should love one another.

JN 13:34

BOB & VICKI

Married 1971

WHAT HAS KEPT YOU JOYFULLY MARRIED FOR 50 OR MORE YEARS?

- ▶ Trying to find something positive every day.

- ▶ Having faith in each other.

- ▶ Having a common mission.

- ▶ Following God's directives and deciding every morning to see the goodness in the world.

I therefore, a prisoner in the
Lord, beseech you that you
walk worthy of the vocation
in which you are called:
With all humility and mildness,
with patience, supporting
one another in charity.

EPH 4:1-2 (DRB)

GEORGE & LINDA

Married 1970

WHAT HAS KEPT YOU JOYFULLY
MARRIED FOR 50 OR MORE YEARS?

- Having a Christ-centered marriage.

- Always listening to each other and coming to an agreement.

- Having a devotion to God helps with being devoted to each other and gives support through difficult times.

COUPLES MARRIED IN THE

1960s

Joy is the serious
business of heaven.
Our merriment must
be between people
who take each
other seriously.

LETTERS TO MALCOLM, CHIEFLY ON PRAYER
C. S. LEWIS[3]

JOE & CINDA

Married 1969

WHAT HAS KEPT YOU JOYFULLY MARRIED FOR 50 OR MORE YEARS?

- ▶ Recognizing the necessity of the presence of God for a joy-filled marriage.

- ▶ Keeping the faith.

- ▶ Knowing that after God the most important relationship in life is with each other.

Joe and Cinda have served in various aspects of marriage ministry for 50 years.

Love is patient, love is kind.
It is not jealous, [love] is not
pompous, it is not inflated, it is not
rude, it does not seek its own
interests, it is not quick-tempered,
it does not brood over injury,
it does not rejoice over wrongdoing
but rejoices with the truth. It bears
all things, believes all things, hopes
all things, endures all things.

1 COR 13:4–7

ARMANDO & LUCIE

Married 1969

WHAT HAS KEPT YOU JOYFULLY MARRIED FOR 50 OR MORE YEARS?

▶ Dialogue.

▶ Having respect.

▶ Knowing that understanding each other is essential.

▶ Being there for each other.

▶ Having lots of love and forgiveness is the key.

Beloved, let us love
one another, because
love is of God;
everyone who loves
is begotten by God
and knows God.

1 JN 4:7

RICHARD & MERRY CAROL

Married 1968

WHAT HAS KEPT YOU JOYFULLY MARRIED FOR 50 OR MORE YEARS?

- ▶ Learning more about each other through the years.

- ▶ Cooling down after fights.

- ▶ Always having a loving outlook.

- ▶ Knowing that mistakes are made.

- ▶ Forgetting the differences and moving on.

- ▶ Starting and ending each day with a kiss.

If there is any encouragement in Christ, any solace in love, any participation in the Spirit, any compassion and mercy, complete my joy by being of the same mind, with the same love, united in heart, thinking one thing.

PHIL 2:1–2

TOM & JUDY

Married 1968

WHAT HAS KEPT YOU JOYFULLY MARRIED FOR 50 OR MORE YEARS?

- ▶ Really, really liking each other and spending time together.

- ▶ Having similar senses of humor and laughing together at the same things.

- ▶ Knowing other couples who are in long-term marriages.

- ▶ Being conservative with money.

If you keep my commandments,
you will remain in my love,
just as I have kept my Father's
commandments and remain in
his love. I have told you this so
that my joy may be in you and
your joy may be complete.

JN 15:10–11

FR. PETER & JUDY

Married 1967

WHAT HAS KEPT YOU JOYFULLY MARRIED FOR 50 OR MORE YEARS?

- Faith.

- Good training; our parents' marriages also lasted more than 50 years.

- Permanent commitment made before God.

- "Each for the other and both for God."

Fr. Peter is a former Episcopal priest who converted with Judy to Catholicism and was subsequently ordained a Catholic priest.

Pessimism is at best an
emotional half-holiday; joy
is the uproarious labour
by which all things live.

ORTHODOXY, G. K. CHESTERTON[4]

KENNY & KAY

Married 1967

WHAT HAS KEPT YOU JOYFULLY MARRIED FOR 50 OR MORE YEARS?

- A sense of humor!

- The ability to laugh at ourselves and not be serious all the time.

- The ability to grow and accept change.

- Total honesty in communication.

- Mutual respect and appreciation.

Love demands effort and a personal commitment to the will of God. It means discipline and sacrifice, but it also means joy and human fulfillment.

SAINT POPE JOHN PAUL II[5]

JOHN & MAUREEN

Married 1967

WHAT HAS KEPT YOU JOYFULLY MARRIED FOR 50 OR MORE YEARS?

- The expectation going into the marriage to stay married.

- The sacrament of marriage and our wedding vows.

- Love for each other through thick and thin.

- Teamwork in completing what needs to get done.

- The vow to each other to stay with it through the ups and downs and everything in between.

- Commitment to each other.

- Learning from our parents' marriages, both of which lasted more than 50 years.

God made us for joy. God
is joy, and the joy of living
reflects the original joy that
God felt in creating us.

SAINT POPE JOHN PAUL II[6]

MALCOLM & PRISCILLA

Married 1966

WHAT HAS KEPT YOU JOYFULLY MARRIED FOR 50 OR MORE YEARS?

- Having faith, staying committed, and persevering when struggles are hard.

- Not giving up.

- Knowing that marriage is for life.

- Having some tough love and trust and working through differences.

- Being determined to make it work.

- Understanding each other more brought more joy through the years.

So faith, hope, love
remain, these three;
but the greatest
of these is love.

1 COR 13:13

BILL & PAULA

Married 1965

WHAT HAS KEPT YOU JOYFULLY MARRIED FOR 50 OR MORE YEARS?

- ▶ Loving each other and being committed to the relationship.

- ▶ Practicing a common faith together.

- ▶ Enjoying a lot of the same things.

- ▶ Holding hands.

- ▶ Even at low points, realizing what a blessing it is to be married to each other.

- ▶ Having harmony and togetherness in the family.

For this is why the gospel was preached even to the dead that, though condemned in the flesh in human estimation, they might live in the spirit in the estimation of God.

The end of all things is at hand. Therefore, be serious and sober for prayers. Above all, let your love for one another be intense, because love covers a multitude of sins.

1 PET 4:6–8

DON & PAULA

Married 1963

WHAT HAS KEPT YOU JOYFULLY
MARRIED FOR 50 OR MORE YEARS?

- Love, forgiveness, and having a lot of patience with each other.

- Not believing in divorce at all; having the intention to stay together and to be married forever.

- Picking the right person.

- Liking each other and being partners.

The fruit of the Spirit
is love, joy, peace,
patience, kindness,
generosity, faithfulness,
gentleness, self-control.

GAL 5:22–23

AL & BARB

Married 1962

WHAT HAS KEPT YOU JOYFULLY MARRIED FOR 50 OR MORE YEARS?

- Love, forgiveness, and patience with each other.

- Taking trips together.

- Having separate hobbies.

- Always talking it out or yelling it out if necessary.

- Not going to bed mad.

- Communicating about everything in life, especially finances and health issues.

May the God of hope fill you with all joy and peace in believing, so that you may abound in hope by the power of the holy Spirit.

ROM 15:13

BRIAN & KATHRYN

Married 1962

WHAT HAS KEPT YOU JOYFULLY MARRIED FOR 50 OR MORE YEARS?

- Growing up in the same religion and attending church together through the years.

- Building memories with each other through a strong faith.

- Being dedicated to each other.

- Going through challenging and fun times as a couple and knowing that the marriage was meant to be.

Come let us praise
the Lord with joy:
let us joyfully sing to
God our saviour.

PS 95:1 (DRB)

DAVID & MARIELO

Married 1962

WHAT HAS KEPT YOU JOYFULLY MARRIED FOR 50 OR MORE YEARS?

- Having a lot of things in common [especially] religion and church.

- Growing in friendship through the years.

- Trying hard through the good and the bad.

No man truly has joy unless he lives in love.

SAINT THOMAS AQUINAS[7]

DON & JUDY

Married 1960

WHAT HAS KEPT YOU JOYFULLY MARRIED FOR 50 OR MORE YEARS?

- ▶ Giving each other a kiss at the start and end of each day.

- ▶ Laughter and love.

- ▶ Doing everything together.

- ▶ Having fun.

- ▶ Talking a lot.

- ▶ Working out the ups and downs.

- ▶ Having children and lots of togetherness in the family.

There is
one and only one
possible road to joy:
selfless love.

PETER KREEFT[8]

JERRY & RITA

Married 1960

WHAT HAS KEPT YOU JOYFULLY MARRIED FOR 50 OR MORE YEARS?

- ▶ Knowing that marriage is for life.

- ▶ Never considering divorce.

- ▶ Making financial and other decisions together.

- ▶ Practicing a common faith together.

- ▶ Being consistent about staying on a budget throughout marriage.

1950s

The fullness of joy is to behold God in all.

JULIAN, ANCHORESS OF NORWICH[9]

CARL & LOIS

Married 1955

WHAT HAS KEPT YOU JOYFULLY MARRIED FOR 50 OR MORE YEARS?

- Being good friends before dating was a big part in the value of the relationship.

- Always having something to discuss and being interested in each other's opinion.

- Both thinking that family and holding the family together are important.

- "The Lord above."

You have made known
to me the paths of life;
you will fill me with joy
in your presence.

ACTS 2:28

LARRY & MARY LOU

Married 1950

WHAT HAS KEPT YOU JOYFULLY MARRIED FOR 50 OR MORE YEARS?

- ▶ Committing to the decision to stay married.

- ▶ Learning to say "Yes, honey."

- ▶ Being and having friends.

- ▶ Staying active.

- ▶ Dancing and going to yacht club parties.

COUPLES MARRIED IN THE

1940s

Joyful, joyful, we adore Thee,
God of glory, Lord of love;

Hearts unfold like flow'rs before Thee,
Op'ning to the sun above.

Melt the clouds of sin and sadness;
Drive the dark of doubt away;

Giver of immortal gladness,
Fill us with the light of day!

"THE HYMN OF JOY"[10]
HENRY VAN DYKE, 1907
(BASED ON PS 71:23)

GEORGE (DEC.) & PAT

Married 1945

WHAT HAS KEPT YOU JOYFULLY MARRIED FOR 50 OR MORE YEARS?

▶ Maintaining an interest in something.

▶ Having a sense of humor and staying curious about things.

▶ Being happy and in love.

▶ Having similar interests.

▶ Each having friends but also having friends together.

▶ Having the same core values, especially about money (how to spend it and not spend it).

George, from the U.S., and Pat, from Australia, met on a blind date. They had the same sense of humor, and he was "a character who matched her character." At the time of George's death, they had been married 67 years.

AFTERWORD

I was praying one afternoon when I was almost finished compiling this book and began to think about the songs that my husband and I chose for our wedding. I smiled as I recalled that our entrance hymn was "Jesu, Joy of Man's Desiring," another was "Joyfully Singing," and the chorus of our recessional hymn was "Rejoice and be glad." The memory seemed to come as a gentle whisper from the Holy Spirit.

While reading and reflecting on all of the couples' responses, I learned key elements for how they have kept their marriages strong: They are committed to their spouse, and they believe in the importance of spending time with each other and doing things together.

A quote from the G. K. Chesterton Society that I came across in my research is what I truly believe happens in loving, committed marriages: "And there is a paradox element to joy, it is best when unexpected."[11]

I encourage you to celebrate couples in your life who have achieved the wonderful milestone of 50 years of marriage and find out what has kept their marriages lasting and joyful.

COUPLES YOU KNOW
WHO HAVE CELEBRATED
50 YEARS OF MARRIAGE

The following pages are for you to add your own notes or words of wisdom from couples you know whose marriages have inspired and encouraged you.

COUPLES YOU KNOW WHO HAVE CELEBRATED 50 YEARS OF MARRIAGE

COUPLES YOU KNOW WHO HAVE CELEBRATED 50 YEARS OF MARRIAGE

COUPLES YOU KNOW WHO HAVE
CELEBRATED 50 YEARS OF MARRIAGE

COUPLES YOU KNOW WHO HAVE CELEBRATED 50 YEARS OF MARRIAGE

REFERENCES

1. *Collins English Dictionary, 12th ed.* (2014), s.v. "joy."

2. William Shakespeare, "Sonnet 8," ed. Amanda Mabillard, *Shakespeare Online*, November 12, 2013, http://www.shakespeare-online.com/sonnets/8.html.

3. C.S. Lewis, *Letters to Malcolm: Chiefly on Prayer.* United Kingdom, Harcourt Brace, 1963, Kindle edition.

4. G. K. Chesterton, *Orthodoxy.* England, Dover Publications, 1908, Kindle edition.

5. Pope John Paul II, "Text of Pope John Paul II's Homily at a Mass on Boston Commons," *The New York Times*, Oct. 2, 1979, https://nyti.ms/3Jh9IYs.

6. Pope John Paul II, AZQuotes.com, accessed January 20, 2022, https://www.azquotes.com/quote/854581.

7. Thomas Aquinas, AZQuotes.com, accessed January 20, 2022, https://www.azquotes.com/quote/1177231.

8. Peter Kreeft, AZQuotes.com, accessed June 15, 2021, https://www.azquotes.com/quote/607657.

9. Julian, Anchoress of Norwich, *Revelations of Divine Love*, Recorded by Julian, Anchoress of Norwich, Anno Domini 1373 (London: Methuen, 1901; Project Gutenberg, 2016), https://www.gutenberg.org/files/52958/52958-h/52958-h.htm.

10. Henry Van Dyke, "The Hymn of Joy" (1907). http://openhymnal.org/Pdf/Joyful_Joyful_We_Adore_Thee-Ode_To_Joy.pdf.

11. G. K. Chesterton, "Chesterton on Joy," Society of G. K. Chesterton, accessed May 2022, https://www.chesterton.org/chesterton-on-joy/.

ABOUT THE AUTHOR

Jeanne Curcio is an author who worked for a number of years as a human factors engineer, technical writer, editor, and French teacher. Throughout her career, she has completed a variety of technical white papers, research projects, and articles that focus on the uniqueness of the human person and the gifts and challenges in life. Being able to blend her love of writing, humanity, and her faith brings her great joy and contentment.

Email Jeanne at:
jeanne.curcio@protonmail.com

Notre Dame de Joie, priez pour nous.
Our Lady of Joy, pray for us.

Printed in the United States
by Baker & Taylor Publisher Services